GREAT SALSAS!

96 Exciting Salsa Recipes

By
Virginia & Robert Hoffman

The Hoffman Press

A few of the recipes in this book appeared in "Salsas," a previous book by Virginia and Robert Hoffman.

Table of Contents

Salsas!

This is a very, very different collection of salsa recipes. This cookbook has the great traditional salsa recipes of Mexico and the Caribbean. You'll find classic salsa recipes from Central and South America...from Africa, Spain, and some that we have created for you.

There are salsas to serve with many kinds of meat, poultry, fish, rice and pasta. There are even salsas for dessert.

Some are very spicy, and some are mild. We'll warn you as to which is which...and we'll tell you how to make them milder...and spicier, too.

Many of the ingredients for traditional salsa recipes are not easily found. We'll tell you where to get them. And if you don't want to do that, we have listed substitutes that are readily available at nearly every supermarket in America.

So, join us in this exciting culinary expedition where you'll use exotic ingredients, encounter new and exciting taste sensations, recall trips to far-off lands, and find pleasure in every recipe.

Virginia Hoffman

Chili Peppers

Here is a simple guide to selecting chilies. (If you know all about chili peppers, skip this and go right on to the recipes).

The names of chili peppers are often confusing. First, they have different names when they are fresh and when they are dried. For example, Jalapeño chilies are called Chipotle chilies when they are dried.

To further complicate matters, chilies have different names in different parts of the country. The Poblano chili, when dried is called Ancho, or Pasillo or Picado chilies, depending upon where you are. Here they are, fresh and dried, with their most commonly used names.

<u>Fresh Chili Peppers</u>

Anaheim or California Chilies are the most commonly found throughout the United States. They are a bright green, with firm flesh, and about six inches long. They are the mildest of all the chili peppers. When canned, they are usually labeled "Green Chilies."

Cayenne Chilies

This is a very, very hot chili pepper. They are very long, thin, and a light green, which turns to a brilliant red when it is mature. Use with care, as the spiciness is not consistently the same, but varies with one chili to another.

Serrano Chilies

These light green chilies are really hot! The canned ones are easier to use, but not quite as intense a flavor.

Jalapeño Chilies

About two or three inches in length, and dark green, these peppers have an unusual feature: the smaller they are, the hotter they are. For convenience sake, you may prefer the canned ones...but use less, as the canned ones pack down in the measuring cup.

Poblano Chilies

These are the chilies that are best for chili relleños (stuffed roasted peppers). A very dark green, almost black, triangular in shape and about two to three inches long. Remember that the darker the pepper, the richer the flavor. Also available dried and canned (look for Ancho chilies).

Red Bell Peppers

These are green bell peppers that have matured and turned red. As is true of the Green ones, the Red are sweet. Because they are so ripe, they have a short shelf life and are often quite expensive. Get the canned ones, or pimientos if you want the sweetness and color at a much lower cost.

Green Bell Peppers

Available the year round in most of the U.S. they are sweet in flavor and may be used in place of some of the spicy chilies to decrease the heat of a recipe.

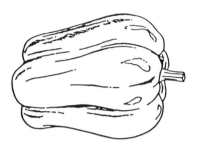

Scotch Bonnet or Habañero Chili Peppers

These are the very hottest of all chili peppers! On a scale of one to ten for heat, a jalapeño would be a five and a Scotch Bonnet or Habañero would be eleven! These chilies must be handled with great care...and the wearing of gloves when handling them. More on the handling later in this book.

Dried Chili Peppers

Ancho chili peppers are also called Pasilla or Picado. These are the dried version names of the Poblano chili, which is ripened before it is dried and is dark mahogany, and large, ranging in flavor from mile to quite snappy. Essential for good Chili Relleños.

Dried Anaheim Chilies are the California or Green Chili pepper, when dried. When smooth skinned, they are mild.

Chipotle is the name for Jalapeño chilies when they are smoke dried after they are thoroughly ripened. Quite unique in flavor, it adds an exciting...and hot taste to any dish.

Japonese is the Serrano chili when ripened and dried. Very, very hot, so use with care.

New Mexico or Red Chilies are generally available only in the dried version. Like the Anaheim pepper in flavor.

Pasilla Chilies are quite mild...except for the seeds, which are really hot.

Pequin or Tepin peppers are a bright red and very tiny. These are the hottest of all the dried chili peppers.

Buying, Preparing and Storing Chili Peppers

When buying fresh chilies, be sure that they have smooth skins with no wrinkles indicating dehydration, and no soft spots. Remember, too, that the smaller the chili is, the hotter it is, so choose the peppers carefully.

A great many recipes call for roasting the chili pepper to remove the skin. If you are doing just one or a few chilies, just use a long-handled fork and hold it a few inches from a top burner on your stove until the pepper has blisters. Remove and peel.

If you have lots of peppers to roast, put them on a non-aluminum baking sheet five or six inches down from the broiling element in your oven, and turn them until they are charred and blistered all over.

Now, place them in a paper bag, not plastic, and leave them for about ten minutes. Remove from bag, and you'll find the skins well loosened. To remove the stems, don't twist them. Just pull gently. If any stems or seeds remain, slit the chili down the side, open and scrape off any seeds or stems remaining.

Dried chilies are often available in lovely wreaths that are colorful in a kitchen. If you buy one, use it for decor. Don't plan on using the peppers for cooking...the open air robs them of their flavor. To store them properly, put them in a cupboard that is cool and dry, or freeze them in small portions in plastic bags.

Warning!

Most chili recipes call for removal of the seeds from the chilies. The seeds of all chili peppers contain a highly irritating oil called Capsicum. If you are preparing one or two chili peppers, you may not need gloves, but we strongly recommend that you wear gloves any time you handle the seeds. And never, never touch your face with your hands when preparing them.

Chili peppers are allergic to aluminum. Strange as it may seem, if you use any aluminum in their preparation—pots funnels, strainers, or aluminum foil—the peppers will acquire a strong metallic flavor that is bitter and completely ruins the salsa. Glass, steel or enamel-coated cookware are fine.

While on the topic of the effects of reactions to the chili pepper, don't store leftover salsas containing chili peppers in plastic containers... unless you want the flavor to remain in the container forever. Use glass or ceramic.

Now, let's make salsas !!!

Blackberry and Onion Salsa

Looking for something different? Use this salsa on your next broiled or barbecued salmon or swordfish.

4 tablespoons olive oil
8 cups thinly sliced red onion
1 jalapeño chili, seeded and minced
1/2 cup red wine
1 cup blackberries (fresh or frozen)
2 teaspoons finely chopped fresh mint
1/2 teaspoon freshly ground black pepper

In olive oil, sauté onions and jalapeño over low heat until coated with oil. Cover pan and cook slowly, stirring frequently, until onions are soft and translucent.

Add wine and blackberries. Cook, mashing them slightly until fruit is well blended. Add mint and black pepper. Stir to blend flavors.

Makes 2 cups.

Cilantro Sauce

A very unusual salsa that is Mexican in its origin, and just great with steaks or hamburgers. Not too hot. Piquant.

4 plum tomatoes, chopped
1 cup chopped cilantro
4 green onions, roughly sliced
1 tablespoon lemon juice
1/4 teaspoon ground cinnamon
1/4 teaspoon ground cumin
2 small green jalapeño chilies, seeded and
    chopped
1/4 teaspoon ground turmeric
1/4 teaspoon ground cloves
Salt and pepper

Process all ingredients in a food processor or blender until a smooth paste forms. Add more lemon juice or a little water to achieve desired consistency.

Makes 1 cup.

A Four-Pepper Salsa

An elegant, colorful salsa to give a special touch to any meal. Equally good, hot or cold.

4 tomatoes, diced
2 fresh jalapeño chilies, roasted*, peeled, seeded and minced
1/2 green bell pepper, chopped
1/2 red bell pepper, chopped
1/2 yellow bell pepper, chopped
1 tablespoon sugar
1 tablespoon olive oil
1 tablespoon wine vinegar
1 tablespoon chopped fresh cilantro
1 tablespoon chopped fresh parsley

Combine all ingredients. Serve at room temperature or chilled.

Makes 2 cups.

*Hold the chilies over gas or electric heat with a long-handled fork. Or, you can blacken them by placing chilies on an oiled cookie sheet under the broiler.

Tomatillo Salsa

This salsa can be powerful! We suggest that you add the hot pepper sauce slowly, and taste it as you go.

1/2 pound tomatillos, husked, rinsed, stemmed
    and cut in large pieces
1 garlic clove, chopped
1/2 teaspoon mustard seed
1-1/2 tablespoons vinegar
1 tablespoon fresh lime juice
2 teaspoons sugar
1 teaspoon white horseradish sauce
2 teaspoons hot pepper sauce

In a food processor, pulse the tomatillos with the garlic and mustard seed until coarsely chopped. Add the vinegar, lime juice, sugar, horseradish and pepper sauce. Process only until blended.

Makes 1 cup.

Black Bean and Avocado Salsa

This is a great salsa spooned on crackers or chips, but try it as an entrée topped with a grilled chicken breast or a beef patty.

2 cups cooked or canned black beans, drained
2 tablespoons olive oil
3 tablespoons fresh lime juice
1/2 cup canned corn kernels
1 ripe avocado, pitted, peeled and diced
1 green bell pepper, seeded and diced
1 red bell pepper, seeded and diced
1/2 cup minced red onion
2 jalapeño chilies, seeded and minced
1/2 teaspoon ground cumin
1/2 cup finely chopped fresh cilantro
Salt and black pepper

Combine all of the ingredients in a mixing bowl. Mix well. Correct seasonings, if necessary, adding salt or lime juice to taste.

Makes 4 cups.

Salsa Naranja De Cuba

Cuba is the source of this orange-based recipe to accompany grilled or barbecued chicken.

2 cups oranges (or mandarin oranges), peeled,
    seeded & diced
1 red onion, diced fine
1/2 red bell pepper, seeded and diced fine
1 tablespoon cumin seeds
1 dried chipotle chili, soaked in warm water
    for 30 minutes, seeded and minced
1/4 cup chopped fresh oregano
1 cup fresh lemon juice
Salt and freshly ground pepper

Mix well in large bowl. Cover and refrigerate.

Makes 4 cups.

Indonesian Peanut Salsa

This is one of the many salsas from Indonesia, and is served over pasta, rice and vegetables.

1 cup finely chopped onion
2 tablespoons vegetable oil
1 teaspoon minced garlic
1 tablespoon minced fresh ginger
1/8 teaspoon cayenne pepper*
1-1/4 cups peanut butter
1 cup water
1/4 cup wine vinegar
1/3 cup soy sauce
1/4 cup lemon juice
1/3 cup molasses

In a heavy-bottomed saucepan, sauté onion in oil until soft. Add garlic, ginger and cayenne.

Using a mixer or food processor, blend peanut butter, water, vinegar, soy sauce, lemon juice and molasses. Combine the two mixtures and simmer until thick.

Makes 2 cups.

*Cayenne pepper makes a medium spicy sauce and may be omitted.

Mint Salsa

This salsa is especially good with lamb and will add zest to barbecued lamb dishes.

1 cup mint leaves, de-stemmed and coarsely
    chopped
2 tablespoons minced onion
2 cloves garlic, minced
1 tablespoon grated fresh ginger root
2 jalapeño chili peppers, seeded and minced
1/4 cup fresh lime juice
1 teaspoon sugar
1/2 teaspoon salt

Place all ingredients in a blender. Blend until you have a smooth sauce. Cover and refrigerate until ready to serve.

Makes 1-1/2 cups.

Tomatillo-Corn Salsa

Serve with barbecued beef or pork.

2 medium tomatillos, husked and chopped
1 cup corn kernels
1 tablespoon minced red onion
1-1/2 teaspoons minced jalapeño pepper
2 tablespoons fresh lime juice
2 tablespoons chopped fresh cilantro
1/2 teaspoon honey
Salt and pepper

Combine all ingredients. Season with salt and pepper. Cover and refrigerate.

Makes 1-1/2 cups.

Golden Salsa

A very mild salsa that is the perfect accompaniment to any large broiled saltwater fish.

1 yellow bell pepper, seeded and diced
2 yellow tomatoes, diced
2 red tomatoes, diced
1/4 cup minced fresh basil
1/4 cup minced fresh parsley
2 teaspoons fresh lime juice
1 teaspoon balsamic vinegar

Combine all ingredients in a bowl.

Makes 2 cups.

Gingered Cranberry Salsa

We think that the people who grow cranberries created this recipe, and we thank them for it. Very tasty!

1 orange, pulp, juice and zest
1 cup whole, fresh cranberries
2 teaspoons grated fresh ginger
2 teaspoons chopped fresh cilantro
2 teaspoons minced jalapeño chilies
1 tablespoon brown sugar
Salt and pepper

Place orange pulp and juice in a food processor; add the cranberries and chop coarsely. Fold in the ginger, cilantro, jalapeños, sugar and zest. Taste, and adjust seasonings if necessary.

Makes 1 cup.

Fresh ginger root is used by the Japanese, Chinese, and people of India to add a peppery spiced and pungent flavor to their food.

Southern Avocado Salsa

Very good topping a salad or baked potato.

2 small ripe avocados, peeled and mashed
1 small ripe tomato, chopped
1/4 cup canned chopped green chilies
1/4 cup minced yellow onion
1/4 cup sour cream
2 tablespoons chopped fresh cilantro
1/2 teaspoon salt
1/4 teaspoon black pepper

In a small bowl, combine all ingredients until well blended. Refrigerate until served.

Makes 1-1/2 cups.

Sweet Tomato Salsa

In the Caribbean, this is served with fish.

2 large ripe tomatoes, diced
1 small red onion, diced
1/4 cup fresh lime juice
1/4 cup chopped cilantro
1 teaspoon cayenne pepper
1 teaspoon toasted cumin seed
Salt and freshly ground pepper

In a medium-sized bowl, combine all ingredients. Mix thoroughly and refrigerate, covered, until ready to serve.

Makes 4 cups.

Salsa De Oaxaca

From the heart of Mexico comes a great salsa for beef fajitas, or any grilled or barbecued beef.

6 plum tomatoes, seeded and diced
1 cup seeded and diced cantaloupe
1 cup seeded and diced watermelon
1 cup peeled and diced cucumber
1/2 cup peeled and chopped red onion
1 small jalapeño chili, seeded and finely minced
2 tablespoons fresh lime juice
2 tablespoons chopped cilantro

In a bowl, mix all ingredients. Let rest at least one hour before serving. Best when served cold.

Makes 4 cups.

San Juan Salsa

The original recipe came from San Juan, Puerto Rico, but we have adapted it so that it's easier to make.

1 tablespoon butter or margarine
1 teaspoon ground cumin
1/4 cup diced onion
1/2 cup canned chopped green chilies
1 16-ounce can ready-cut peeled tomatoes
1 cup crushed unsweetened canned pineapple
1/4 cup lime juice
1/8 teaspoon ground cinnamon
Salt and pepper

Melt the butter in a saucepan, adding cumin, onion and chili peppers when hot. Sauté until onion is translucent. Add tomatoes, pineapple, lime juice and cinnamon.

Simmer for 5 minutes. Add salt and pepper if desired. Cook and serve at room temperature.

Makes 3 cups.

27

Roasted Corn and Chili Salsa

Barbecuing? Here's the ideal accompaniment for meat, chicken, turkey and ham.

4 ears corn, husked
1 tablespoon vegetable oil
1 teaspoon salt
1/4 teaspoon freshly ground black pepper
4 scallions, ends removed and thinly sliced
1 red bell pepper, roasted*, seeded and diced fine
1 jalapeño chili, seeded and minced

Rub the corn lightly with the vegetable oil and sprinkle with salt and pepper. Grill over a low fire until they're slightly charred, about 10 minutes.

Remove the corn from the grill. Cool and slice the kernels off the cobs. In a large bowl, mix the corn kernels with the remaining ingredients. Keep covered and refrigerated.

Makes about 3 cups.

*Hold the pepper over gas or electric heat with a long-handled fork. Or, pepper can be blackened by placing on an oiled cookie sheet under the broiler.

Smooth Picante Salsa

While you may use this salsa in many ways, it is particularly good with chicken and turkey.

1 tablespoon olive oil
1 medium onion, diced
1 red bell pepper, seeded and diced
2 stalks of celery, cut into 1-inch lengths
1 can (8 ounces) tomato sauce
2 small poblano chilies, seeded and chopped

Heat olive oil in medium pan. Add onion and cover for 3 minutes. Add pepper and celery; cook for an additional 5 minutes, then add rest of ingredients.

Cook all ingredients together, simmering for 15 to 20 minutes. Add water, if necessary. Allow to cool. Place in blender and blend until smooth. Reheat to serve.

Makes 1-1/2 cups.

Mediterranean Vegetable Salsa

Spain is the birthplace of this salsa that is served with broiled chicken, or simply spooned on coarse farm bread.

3 tablespoons olive oil
1/2 cup finely chopped onion
3 cloves garlic, minced
2 green onions (white and part green), sliced thin
2 medium carrots, chopped fine
2 medium zucchini, chopped fine
1/2 tablespoon lemon juice
1/2 teaspoon lemon zest
3 oil-packed, sun-dried tomatoes, chopped
2 tablespoons finely chopped fresh basil

In olive oil, sauté onions and garlic over low heat until they begin to soften. Add green onions, carrots and zucchini. Cook slowly until tender.

Stir in lemon juice, zest and sun-dried tomatoes. Cook briefly, stirring, to blend flavors. Add basil at the last minute. Add salt if desired. Serve warm.

Makes 2 cups.

Velvety Gazpacho Salsa

Use this salsa with chicken breasts pounded to an even thickness, barbecued for 5 minutes on each side, or topping a hamburger.

5 tomatillos, husked, rinsed and diced
1/2 cup virgin olive oil
1-1/2 tablespoons fresh lime juice
1/3 cup vinegar
2 tablespoons chopped fresh cilantro
1 avocado, pitted, peeled and diced
1/2 red onion, peeled and diced
2 large plum tomatoes, diced
1/2 cucumber, peeled and diced
2 serrano chilies, seeded and minced
1 red bell pepper, seeded and diced
Salt

In a blender or food processor, purée tomatillos, oil, lime juice, vinegar, cilantro and avocado. Add remaining ingredients and purée again.

Makes 3 cups.

Corn and Avocado Salsa

This very mild salsa can be "heated" easily by substituting a jalapeño for the green chilies.

2 cups fresh corn (cut from 3 ears)
3/4 cup finely chopped onion
3/4 cup cider vinegar
2 tablespoons sugar
1-1/2 teaspoons salt
2 firm-ripe avocados
2 tablespoons diced pimiento
1 tablespoon diced green chilies

In a saucepan, combine corn, onion, vinegar, sugar and salt. Boil for 5 minutes, stirring occasionally. Cool completely. Set aside.

Peel and pit the avocados. In a bowl, mash one of the avocados. Chop the remaining avocado into small cubes and add to the mashed avocado. Add the drained corn mixture and 3 tablespoons of the cooking liquid, along with the pimiento and green chilies. Toss to combine well. Cover and refrigerate.

Makes 3 cups.

Melon Salsa

A perfect salsa for serving with shrimp, crab or any mild fish.

1 cup diced ripe cantaloupe
1 cup diced ripe watermelon
1 cup diced, peeled and seeded cucumber
5 ripe plum tomatoes, seeded and diced
1/2 cup minced onion
2 tablespoons chopped fresh parsley
2 teaspoons seeded, minced jalapeño chili pepper
2 tablespoons fresh lime juice

Combine all the ingredients in a bowl. Cover and refrigerate one hour before serving to allow flavors to blend.

Makes 4 cups.

It's easy to grow your own fresh chilies. Most nurseries, garden centers, and seed companies have them.

Pico De Gallo Salsa #1

The name of this classic Vera Cruz recipe means "Rooster's Beak" or "Sharp Bite"!

4 medium tomatoes, chopped
6 green onions with half of the green tops, chopped
3 jalapeño chilies, seeded and chopped fine
1-1/2 tablespoons vegetable oil
1/3 cup chopped cilantro

Blend thoroughly. Chill before serving.

Makes 2 cups.

Pico De Gallo Salsa #2

This is a variation of the classic recipe, this time featuring serrano chilies and radishes. Hotter than #1!

2 tomatoes, diced
1/2 cup diced onion
6 radishes, stemmed and diced
3 tablespoons chopped cilantro
3 serrano chilies, seeded and diced
1 tablespoon lime juice

Combine all ingredients. Chill and serve.

Makes 2 cups.

Pico De Gallo Salsa #3

This version uses fruit as its base, instead of vegetables.

1/2 cup seeded and diced watermelon
1 cup peeled and diced jicama
1 orange, peeled, seeded and diced
1 jalapeño chili, seeded and diced
2 tablespoons chopped fresh cilantro
1 tablespoon lime juice

Mix all ingredients. Serve chilled.

Makes 3 cups.

Salsa Verde

This is your basic salsa verde (green salsa). It takes just minutes to make.

2 cups canned tomatillos, drained
1 clove garlic, crushed
2 cans diced jalapeño chilies
1/2 cup finely chopped fresh cilantro

Place all ingredients in a blender or food processor and process until will blended. Refrigerate for several hours.

Makes 2 cups.

Apple-Mango Salsa

A tasty combination with a crunch!

1 Granny Smith apple, peeled and diced
2 firm-ripe mangoes, peeled and cut into
   1/4-inch dice
1 medium onion, chopped fine
3 tablespoons fresh lime juice
4 garlic cloves, minced
2 fresh jalapeño chilies, seeded and minced
1/4 cup chopped fresh cilantro
Pinch of cumin
Salt and pepper

Combine apple, mangoes and other ingredients in a bowl. Mix together. Season salsa with salt and pepper. Cover.

Makes about 3 cups.

Summer Melon Salsa

A favorite in the Wine Country. Serve it with chips or over grilled chicken, turkey or pork.

3 kiwis, chopped small
1 small red onion, chopped fine
4 tomatillos, husked, rinsed and chopped fine
2 medium tomatoes, chopped fine
1 ripe melon (cantaloupe, honeydew or
    crenshaw), diced
Juice of 1 lemon
Juice of 1 lime
4 tablespoons peanut oil
2 bunches fresh cilantro, stemmed and
    chopped
2 jalapeño chilies, seeded and minced
Salt and pepper

Combine all ingredients in a large bowl. Stir well.
Makes 4 to 5 cups.

Havana Salsa

Miami's Cuban community gets homesick when this is served. It is really authentic.

2 cups peeled, seeded and diced ripe papaya
1 cup cooked black beans
1/4 cup finely chopped red onion
2 jalapeño chilies, seeded and minced
2 teaspoons minced fresh ginger
1/4 cup chopped cilantro
3 tablespoons fresh lime juice
1 tablespoon olive oil
1 tablespoon light brown sugar
Salt and freshly ground pepper

Combine all of the ingredients in a bowl, and gently toss to mix. Cover and refrigerate until served.

Makes 4 cups.

Italian Green Salsa

This piquant herb and olive oil sauce is especially good with shrimp or fish.

2 garlic cloves, minced
2 tablespoons minced parsley
2 tablespoons minced fresh chives
2 tablespoons minced pimiento
1 teaspoon capers
1/4 teaspoon black pepper
Salt to taste
1/2 cup olive oil
1/2 cup fresh lime juice

In a small bowl, combine the garlic, parsley, chives, pimiento and capers. Whisk in the oil and lime juice. Season with salt and pepper. Cover and set aside. Best served at room temperature.

Makes 2 cups.

Mexican Melon Salsa

The delicate flavor of the melons and jicama is brought to life with the red pepper flakes.

1-1/2 cups peeled and diced jicama
3/4 cup peeled and diced ripe papaya
1 jalapeño chili, seeded and minced
1 teaspoon dried red pepper flakes
1/2 cup lime juice
1/4 teaspoon salt
1/2 cup chopped cilantro leaves
2 cups peeled and diced honeydew melon
2 cups peeled and diced cantaloupe

In a large bowl, combine jicama, papaya and jalapeño. Add the lime juice and salt to coat. Add cilantro, red pepper flakes and melons; toss. Cover and refrigerate until ready to serve.

Makes 6 cups.

Cranberry Apricot Salsa

*Remember this recipe for holiday entertaining—
a great accompaniment to roast turkey, chicken
or pork.*

2 tablespoons butter
2 jalapeño chilies, seeded and minced
1/2 cup minced red onion
2 tablespoons minced fresh ginger
4 cups fresh or frozen cranberries
2 cups fresh orange juice
1/2 cup light brown sugar
1/2 pound dried apricots, chopped
1 tablespoon curry powder
Salt and pepper.

Melt the butter in a saucepan over medium heat.
Add the jalapeños, onion, ginger and 2 cups of
the cranberries. Cook for 5 minutes, or until the
cranberries have popped.

Increase the heat to high, add the orange juice
and brown sugar. Bring to a boil. Reduce heat to
medium and simmer for 10 minutes. Add the
remaining 2 cups of the cranberries, the apricots,
curry powder, salt and pepper. Mix well and simmer
for 5 minutes. Remove the pan from heat. Cool
at room temperature. Pour the mixture into a
glass bowl, cover and refrigerate.

Makes 5 cups

Fresh Seafood Salsa

This salsa is particularly good with broiled or barbecued seafood.

2 tomatoes, peeled and chopped
1/2 cup diced onion
2 cloves garlic, crushed
2 red bell peppers, seeded and chopped
1 jalapeño chili, seeded and chopped
2 teaspoons lemon juice
1 tablespoon chopped fresh cilantro
2 tablespoons olive oil

Place all ingredients except olive oil in blender and pulse until quite smooth. Heat olive oil on medium heat, and add to the blender mixture; mix well.

Makes 1 cup.

Columbus is responsible for the name of "Pepper" for chilies. He thought they were pepper seeds when he brought them back from the New World.

Easy Roasted Corn Salsa

Make this when you have extra time for cooking and want to have a truly different salsa. Serve as a side dish.

4 cups fresh corn kernels, or 2 10-ounce
   packages frozen corn, thawed and drained
1 tablespoon chili powder
2 teaspoons ground cumin
4 medium ripe tomatoes, diced
3/4 cup finely chopped red onion
1/2 cup chopped fresh cilantro
2 small jalapeño chilies, seeded and minced
1 clove garlic, chopped fine
1 tablespoon olive oil
1 tablespoon cider vinegar
1 teaspoon salt
Pepper

Heat oven to 400 degrees. Combine the corn, chili powder and cumin in a large bowl. Spread out mixture evenly on a greased 15 x 10-inch cookie sheet. Bake for 25 minutes, stirring occasionally, until corn is lightly browned. Cool.

Stir together tomatoes, onion, cilantro, jalapeño, garlic, oil, vinegar, salt and pepper in a large bowl. Stir in corn. Cover and refrigerate until ready to serve.

Makes 5 to 6 cups.

Harvest Tomato Salsa

If you have an over-abundance of tomatoes, this is the ideal way to preserve them—Make-Ahead Salsa.

5 pounds tomatoes, peeled and chopped
1 green bell pepper, seeded and chopped
1/2 cup diced onion
1 can (4 ounces) diced jalapeño chilies
1 cup brown sugar
1 cup wine vinegar
1 tablespoon cinnamon
1 teaspoon cumin

Simmer tomatoes, bell pepper and onion for one hour. Then add remaining ingredients, stirring well. Simmer for 30 minutes. Cool slightly and purée in blender or food processor.

Freeze in one-cup portions. When ready to use, thaw in microwave or conventional oven, and heat before serving. Double or triple the quantities if you have lots of tomatoes.

Makes 5 cups.

Fresh Corn Salsa

Corn is universal in the Islands and Latin America. This salsa is best when made with fresh corn just cooked.

4 ears fresh corn, shucked
1 cup diced zucchini
3 tablespoons olive oil
3 medium tomatoes, diced
1 serrano chili, seeded and minced
1 medium onion, diced
1/2 cup chopped fresh cilantro
2 tablespoons lime juice
1/2 teaspoon ground cumin
1 cup tomato sauce or catsup

Boil the corn for 2 to 3 minutes. When cool, cut off the cob. In a skillet, sauté the zucchini in olive oil until skin is bright green, but still crisp. Remove from heat.

In a bowl, combine tomatoes, chili, onion, cilantro, lime juice, cumin and tomato sauce.

Stir in the corn kernels and zucchini. Mix well; cover and refrigerate for one hour or more. Serve cold.

Makes 5 to 6 cups.

Great Salsas!

Salsa Immediatemente!

Salsa in seconds with this recipe. Serve it as a dip for chips, toastettes, or pita rounds.

4 medium tomatoes, chopped
1 can diced green chilies
1/4 cup finely chopped onion
1/4 cup chopped fresh cilantro

Mix well. Serve chilled or at room temperature.
Makes 1 cup.

Hot Mango Salsa

Fresh mangoes, the key to salsas in the West Indies, are available in most supermarkets.

4 medium fresh, ripe mangoes, peeled, pitted
    and chopped
1/4 cup chopped fresh cilantro
1 small red onion, chopped
2 jalapeño chilies, seeded and minced
1/4 cup lime juice
Salt and pepper

Combine all ingredients in a bowl. Add salt and pepper to taste.

Makes 2 cups.

Salsa Cruda

This recipe for classic salsa cruda for true salsa lovers is better if made a day ahead.

1-1/2 jalapeño chilies, seeded and cored
1 tablespoon minced garlic
1 cup minced scallions
4 ripe tomatoes, seeded and cut in large
    pieces
Juice of 1 lime
1/2 cup stemmed and coarsely chopped fresh
    cilantro
3/4 teaspoon salt
1/4 teaspoon freshly ground pepper

In a food processor fitted with a steel blade, add jalapeño and garlic. Pulse until a fine paste is formed. Add the scallions, pulsing on and off several times. Add the tomatoes. Chop until fine, pulsing on and off.

Transfer mixture to a serving bowl; stir in the lemon juice, cilantro, salt and pepper. To blend flavors, cover and let sit for 30 minutes at room temperature.

Makes 3 cups.

Mixed Vegetable Salsa

A very attractive salsa, to be served as a relish alongside your meat, fish or poultry entrée.

4 tomatoes, diced
1 zucchini squash, diced
1 yellow squash, diced
1 jar (4 ounces) diced pimiento
2 small jalapeño or serrano chilies, seeded
    and chopped fine
2 tablespoons olive oil
2 tablespoons lime juice
1/3 cup chopped fresh cilantro

Mix all ingredients well and store in refrigerator overnight.

Makes 2 cups.

Remember, the smaller the chili, the hotter it is.

Salsa of Kingston

Jamaica is the source for this recipe for halibut, swordfish, mahi mahi and tuna.

1 small pineapple, peeled, cored and diced
2 kiwi fruit, peeled and diced
1 mango, peeled and diced
1 medium papaya, peeled and diced
1 cup cooked black beans, rinsed
1/4 poblano chili, seeded and diced
1/2 cup raspberry vinegar
1/4 cup dark rum
2 tablespoons brown sugar
Juice of 2 limes
1/2 cup chopped cilantro
Salt

Combine all of the salsa ingredients. Refrigerate until ready to serve.

Makes 2 to 3 cups.

Cranberry Salsa

Perfect for the holidays, this salsa was created to go with Thanksgiving and Christmas turkey.

1 large red apple, preferably Delicious
1 large orange, including rind
1 pound fresh cranberries
2 tablespoons lemon juice
2 cups sugar
2 jalapeño chilies, seeded and minced

Core and seed apple and cut into chunks. Seed the orange and cut into chunks. Wash cranberries thoroughly, removing any spoiled ones.

Put apple, orange with rind and cranberries in a food processor and chop together. Stir in lemon juice, sugar and jalapeño chilies, and mix very well.

Make this salsa at least two days before you plan on using it. It freezes well and makes a great holiday gift.

Makes 3 cups.

Hot Sesame Salsa

Sesame oil gives a unique flavor to this salsa. It is available in most supermarkets or specialty food stores.

2 tablespoons sesame oil
1/2 cup chopped onions
1/2 cup chopped fresh jalapeño chilies
2 garlic cloves, minced
6 cups chopped tomatoes
1 tablespoon crushed red peppers
2 tablespoons wine vinegar
1 tablespoon sesame seeds, toasted

Heat oil in a saucepan. Add onions, jalapeños and garlic. Sauté for 3 minutes until the onions are translucent. Add the tomatoes. Cover and cook until tomatoes are broken, 10 to 15 minutes.

Place cooked mixture in a good processor fitted with a steel blade, or blender, and process quickly. It should remain slightly chunky.

Return sauce to the pan and add the rest of the ingredients. Simmer for 5 to 7 minutes. Refrigerate to store.

Makes 2 cups.

Authoritative Salsa

In El Salvador, the term "Tiene Autoridad" is often applied to a dish that speaks for itself. This salsa does!

3 ripe tomatoes, chopped fine
2 jalapeño chilies, seeded, cored and minced
1 medium red onion, chopped fine
10 sprigs fresh cilantro, chopped
1/2 teaspoon salt
3 tablespoons fresh lime juice
3 tablespoons fresh orange juice
1/2 teaspoon freshly grated orange zest

Combine tomatoes, chilies, onion and cilantro in a bowl. Stir in the salt, lime juice, orange juice and zest. Let sit for at least 30 minutes before serving. Keep covered and refrigerated.

Makes about 2 cups.

It is said that several thousand years ago, the Mayans had the first chili farms in Central America.

Parsley Salsa

A really tasty salsa for boiled beef, cold roast beef, or on sliced tomatoes.

1/2 cup minced fresh curly-leaf parsley
2 tablespoons minced pimiento
1/4 cup chopped toasted almonds
1/3 cup olive oil
2 tablespoons wine vinegar
1/4 teaspoon salt
1/8 teaspoon black pepper

Combine all ingredients in a glass bowl. Mix well. Cover and refrigerate. Serve cold.

Makes 1 cup.

Spanish Garlic Salsa

A recipe from Spain for garlic lovers. Serve over rice or pasta or as a bread dip.

2/3 cup olive oil
4 cloves garlic, pressed
4 tablespoons lime juice
2 tablespoons lemon juice
1 teaspoon dried oregano
1 teaspoon dried cilantro

Combine all ingredients and mix well. Serve immediately.

Makes 1 cup.

Michoacan Salsa Cruda

There are many, many salsa cruda recipes. This one is from Michoaca, Mexico.

1 medium yellow onion, peeled and minced
3 fresh ripe tomatoes, peeled and coarsely
   chopped
2 tablespoons minced cilantro
1 clove garlic, minced
1 small green chili, minced
1 tablespoon fresh lime juice
Salt

One hour before serving, combine all ingredients, except salt. Do not add salt until the last minute. This salsa is best when freshly made.

Makes 3/4 cup.

"Ristras" are strings of dried red chilies hung in doorways to keep evil spirits away.

Tomato and Chipotle Salsa

A bit of work to blacken the tomatoes, but the resulting salsa is well worth the effort.

1/4 cup plus 1 tablespoon olive oil
1/2 large onion, chopped
4 blackened ripe Roma tomatoes*
4 teaspoons minced garlic
1/2 cup minced fresh cilantro
2 tablespoons diced and canned chipotle
   peppers
4 Roma tomatoes, peeled, seeded and chopped
1/4 cup red wine vinegar
1 tablespoon salt
1 teaspoon sugar

In food processor, place onion, blackened tomatoes and garlic. Pulse until finely chopped, but not puréed. Add cilantro and chilies. Pulse to mix. Add seeded Roma tomatoes, remaining 1/4 cup oil, vinegar, salt and sugar to mixture. Stir until combined.

Makes 3 cups.

*Place tomatoes on an oiled cookie sheet under the broiler until blackened and soft. Then chop with peel.

Vera Cruz Lime Salsa

This is particularly good when served as a relish with fish.

2 large tomatoes, chopped
2 large tomatillos, husked, washed and
  chopped fine
1/3 cup finely chopped red onion
1/3 cup seeded and finely chopped red bell
  pepper
2 tablespoons fresh lime juice
2 tablespoons grated lime peel

Mix together all ingredients. Cover and refrigerate overnight.   Makes 2 cups.

Salsa De Diablo

This is a serious salsa! Proceed with caution.

8 tomatoes, chopped
1 small onion, chopped
2 Anaheim chilies, seeded and diced
2 serrano chilies, seeded and diced
2 tablespoons olive oil
2 tablespoons wine vinegar
1 teaspoon fresh minced garlic
1/4 teaspoon ground pepper

Mix well, and serve chilled.   Makes 4 cups.

Easy Black Bean Salsa

Barbecued or grilled pork chops take on a new dimension when this salsa is served as a condiment.

1 can (15 ounces) black beans, drained
1 tablespoon olive oil
1/2 cup diced pimiento
1/8 teaspoon cumin
1/2 cup chopped fresh cilantro
4 green onions, chopped fine
1 tablespoon lime juice

Mix well and chill.

Makes 2-1/2 cups.

Steakhouse Salsa

You've seen bowls of it in fancy and not-so-fancy steakhouses for years. Here's the recipe.

4 ripe tomatoes, coarsely chopped
2 cans diced green chilies
2 tablespoons chopped fresh cilantro
1 medium onion, chopped
1/2 teaspoon sugar
1 tablespoon vinegar

Mix together well and refrigerate for two hours before serving.

Makes 3 cups.

Fresh Peach Salsa

Only fresh, ripe peaches will do to make this summer salsa. Great with tortilla chips, fish or chicken.

4 fresh peaches, peeled and chopped (about
    2 cups)
1/2 cup chopped sweet onion
3 tablespoons lime juice
2 tablespoons fresh jalapeño chilies, seeded
    and chopped fine
1 clove garlic, minced
1 tablespoon chopped fresh cilantro
1/2 teaspoon sugar

In a medium glass mixing bowl, stir together peaches, onion, lime juice, peppers, garlic, cilantro and sugar. Cover and chill for one to two hours.

                                        Makes 2 cups.

Golden Raspberry Salsa

If you use golden raspberries, use the yellow bell pepper. If you use red raspberries, use a red bell pepper.

1 pint gold or red raspberries, coarsely
   chopped
1/4 cup finely diced red onion
2 tablespoons fresh orange juice
1/4 cup finely diced yellow bell pepper
2 tablespoons lime juice
2 tablespoons chopped fresh cilantro
1 jalapeño chili, seeded and diced fine
Salt

Combine salsa ingredients in a glass bowl. Cover and refrigerate until ready to use.

Makes 2 cups.

Dried chilies have been used as a medicine for centuries in most civi - lizations where they were available.

Olive and Jalapeño Salsa

The chopped green olives give this salsa a distinctive flavor.

1 tablespoon olive or canola oil
3/4 cup finely chopped jalapeños
2 garlic cloves, minced
1/4 cup finely chopped onion
3 cups peeled, seeded and chopped tomatoes
1 tablespoon red wine vinegar
1 tablespoon chopped fresh cilantro
2 tablespoons chopped green olives

Heat oil in a medium-sized skillet. Add the jalapeños, garlic and onion. Sauté until the onion is translucent. Add the tomatoes and cook until they are soft. Add remaining ingredients and stir, cooking 5 minutes more. Stir well before serving.

Makes 2 cups.

If you prefer a milder salsa, used one-half sweet green bell peppers and one-half jalapeño chilies.

Orange and Tomato Salsa

A recipe from Haiti to serve with grilled fish or chicken.

3 oranges, peeled, white pith removed, seeded and diced
1-1/2 cups chopped seeded tomatoes
1/4 cup minced onion
1/4 cup chopped fresh parsley
2 teaspoons minced garlic
1 teaspoon minced peeled fresh ginger
1/8 teaspoon cayenne pepper
Salt
2 tablespoons fresh orange juice
2 teaspoons balsamic vinegar

Combine all ingredients in a glass bowl. Season to taste with pepper and salt. Cover and refrigerate for at least one hour. Bring to room temperature before serving.

Makes 4 cups.

Sweet-Sour Salsa

Costa Rica is the source of this sweet and sour salsa. Serve with toastettes, crackers or toasted pita quarters.

1 fresh pineapple, peeled, cored and diced
1/4 cup minced red onion
1 red bell pepper, cored, seeded and diced
1 jalapeño chili, seeded and minced
1/2 cup chopped fresh cilantro
3 tablespoons fresh lime juice
1 tablespoon dark brown sugar
Salt and freshly ground pepper

Combine all the ingredients in a large bowl; mix well. Correct seasonings, if needed, by adding salt, sugar or lime juice to taste.

Makes 2 to 3 cups.

Papaya Salsa

From Hawaii comes this salsa, used there in luaus with roast pig, and nearly as good with pork roasted in a gas or electric oven.

3 cups diced ripe papaya
3 ripe tomatoes, diced
1 cup chopped red bell pepper
1-1/2 cups chopped red onion
1 jalapeño chili, seeded and minced
2 teaspoons ground cumin
2 tablespoons olive oil
2 tablespoons red wine vinegar
1/2 cup freshly squeezed lime juice
1 teaspoon ground black pepper
1 teaspoon bottled hot pepper sauce
1 cup chopped fresh cilantro

Combine all ingredients in a large bowl. Toss thoroughly. Serve chilled or at room temperature.

Makes 5 cups.

63

Green Tomato Salsa

Yes, it's a great dip, but it's even better when served with barbecued or broiled pork or lamb.

1 poblano chili, roasted*, peeled, cored, seeded and chopped
4 to 5 green tomatoes, seeded and chopped
1 jalapeño chili, cored, seeded and minced
2 tablespoons chopped fresh cilantro
1/2 teaspoon ground cumin
2 tablespoons red wine vinegar
1 medium red onion, diced (approximately 1/2 cup)

Mix all ingredients in a large bowl. Serve at room temperature.

Makes 2 cups.

Hold the chilies over gas or electric heat with a long-handled fork to roast.

Pineapple-Carrot Salsa

A nice, mild salsa that you can serve anyone!

2 cups coarsely grated carrots
2 cups crushed (canned) pineapple, drained
   (save juice)
1/4 cup golden raisins
1/4 cup minced mild onion
1/4 cup finely chopped red bell pepper
2 tablespoons minced fresh cilantro
1/2 jalapeño chili pepper, seeded and minced
1/4 cup (4 tablespoons) fresh lime juice

Soak raisins in 1/4 cup juice drained from pineapple; put aside.

In a medium-sized glass bowl, combine carrots and drained pineapple. Add the raisins, onions, red bell pepper, cilantro, chili pepper and lime juice. Mix well. Cover and marinate in refrigerator for at least one hour before serving.

Makes 4 to 5 cups.

Salsa De Manzana (Apple)

Serve with roast pork or ham.

2 large Golden Delicious apples, peeled,
    cored and cut in cubes
1/4 cup fresh lime juice
1/4 cup minced onion
1/4 cup chopped fresh cilantro
1 Anaheim chili pepper, seeded and finely
    chopped
1 red chili pepper, seeded and finely chopped
1 tablespoon grated fresh ginger
1/2 cup fresh seedless grapes, cut in half

Place apple cubes in a glass bowl with lime juice.
Toss to preserve apple color. Add all remaining
ingredients and mix well. Cover and refrigerate
until ready to serve.

Makes 2 to 2-1/2 cups.

Fresh Chili-Cherry Salsa

This savory salsa adds a new taste experience with grilled chicken or pork.

1-1/2 cups fresh bing cherries, pitted and
    chopped (approximately 1 pound)
1/4 cup finely diced red bell pepper
3 tablespoons minced onion
1 jalapeño chili pepper, seeded and minced
2 tablespoons fresh lime juice
1/4 teaspoon salt
1/2 cup diced ripe mango
1 tablespoon fresh basil

Combine cherries, peppers, onion and lime juice in bowl. Add salt and let stand for 10 to 15 minutes before adding mango and basil. Serve at room temperature for best flavor.

Makes 2-1/4 cups.

Pineapple-Pepper Salsa

This is a mild recipe for the faint of heart. If you are braver, add more jalapeños.

1 large pineapple, peeled and cored
1-1/2 cups seeded and finely chopped red
   bell pepper
1/2 cup finely chopped red onion
1 jalapeño chili, seeded and minced
1/3 cup wine vinegar
2 tablespoons sugar
1 teaspoon salt
1/4 cup chopped fresh cilantro

Dice the pineapple and put in a bowl. Toss with the bell pepper, red onion, and jalapeño. Add the vinegar, sugar, salt and cilantro. Mix well. Refrigerate for two to three hours.To blend flavors, mix several times during this period.

Makes about 3 cups.

Summer Papaya-Kiwi Salsa

This American-born salsa combines the papaya of the Caribbean and the kiwi of New Zealand.

1 small firm-ripe papaya, peeled, seeded
  and diced
2 kiwi fruit, peeled and diced
3 tablespoons lemon juice
2 tablespoons lime juice
1 medium red bell pepper, seeded and diced
1 medium yellow bell pepper, seeded and
  diced
2 fresh jalapeño chilies, seeded and diced
2 tablespoons sugar

In a bowl, gently mix papaya, kiwi, lemon juice, lime juice, red pepper, yellow pepper, jalapeños and sugar. Serve, or cover and chill up to four hours. Serve with grilled fish or chicken.

Makes 2 cups.

The kiwi fruit is now cultivated extensively in both New Zealand and California.

Nectarine Salsa

Summer is the time for this salsa, with fresh nectarines as its base. Spoon it over grilled or broiled chicken.

4 nectarines, peeled and diced
1/4 cup seeded and diced red bell pepper
1/2 cup finely chopped red onion
1 tablespoon minced garlic
1 small jalapeño chili, seeded and minced
2 tablespoons minced scallions
3 tablespoons chopped cilantro
3 tablespoons orange juice
1-1/2 teaspoons honey
Salt and freshly ground black pepper

Combine the ingredients in a bowl. Add salt and pepper to taste.

Makes about 2-1/2 cups.

Tropical Banana Salsa

This salsa is a little sweet, a little sour. Just right for barbecued or grilled fish of any kind, and shrimp, too.

2 large bananas, peeled and diced
1/2 cup seeded and minced red bell pepper
1/2 cup seeded and minced green bell pepper
1 jalapeño chili, seeded and minced
1 tablespoon minced fresh ginger
3 scallions, chopped fine
1/4 cup chopped fresh cilantro
3 tablespoons chopped fresh cilantro
3 tablespoons fresh lime juice
2 tablespoons brown sugar
1/4 teaspoon ground cardamom
1 tablespoon olive oil
Salt and freshly ground pepper

Combine all of the ingredients in a bowl and gently toss to mix. Correct the seasonings if needed, adding salt, lime juice or sugar. The salsa should be sweet and sour.

Refrigerate, covered, until serving time. For best flavor, serve within two hours of making.

Makes 3 cups.

Easy No-Cook Salsa

This salsa could be heated and served as a vegetable with barbecued chicken.

1 can (11 ounces) whole-kernel corn, drained
1 can (8 ounces) creamed corn
1 4-ounce jar diced pimiento
1/2 cup minced mild red onion
1 can (4 ounces) diced green chilies
2 tablespoons wine vinegar

Mix all ingredients in a medium-sized glass bowl. Cover and refrigerate. Best served at room temperature.

Makes 4 cups.

Chilies were one of the first plants cultivated in the New World.

Grilled Tomatillo Salsa

6 medium fresh tomatillos
2 Anaheim chilies
2 tablespoons fresh lime juice
2 cloves garlic, crushed
1/4 cup chopped onion
1/2 teaspoon salt
1 teaspoon sugar
2 jalapeño chilies
1/4 cup chopped cilantro

Remove the husks from the tomatillos and rinse. Broil tomatillos and chilies until charred, about 8 to 10 minutes. Steam chilies for approximately 15 minutes in a covered bowl. Core the tomatillos; place in food processor. Process until almost puréed.

Remove the seeds and cores from the Anaheim chilies, but do not remove their charred skin. Chop finely. Combine with tomatillos. Add all other ingredients except the jalapeño chilies and cilantro. Stir well and taste. Correct seasoning. Seed and mince jalapeños. Add to the salsa, along with the cilantro. Stir well. Cover and refrigerate.

Makes 3 to 4 cups.

Grilled Corn Salsa

Serve this rolled up in flour tortillas, or with scrambled eggs for a Sunday brunch.

3 medium-sized ears of corn, husked
2 Anaheim chilies
1 can (16 ounces) black beans, rinsed and drained
3 plum tomatoes, chopped
2 tablespoons fresh lemon juice
1 tablespoon fresh lime juice
1/4 teaspoon each salt and pepper

Peel, core and seed chilies. Chop fine.

Mix all ingredients in a bowl. Serve at room temperature.

Makes 4 cups.

Mexicorn Salsa

This colorful salsa tastes as good as it looks. Serve it as a vegetable with hamburgers or meatloaf.

3 tablespoons oil
2 tablespoons flour
1/4 cup chopped red bell pepper
1 can (4 ounces) diced green chilies
1/4 teaspoon dry mustard
2 cups tomato juice
1 can (15 ounces) whole kernel Mexicorn,
    drained

Heat oil, stir in flour and mix until flour is absorbed. Add remaining ingredients, except corn, and simmer slowly until mixture thickens, about 10 minutes. Remove from heat, add corn and serve.

Makes 3 cups.

Low in fat and calories and high in fiber, salsa is ideal for dieters.

A Three-Pepper Salsa

A simple, easy-to-make and attractive salsa. No cooking, just dicing, chopping and enjoying.

1 red bell pepper, seeded and diced
1 yellow bell pepper, seeded and diced
1 jalapeño chili, seeded and minced
1 clove garlic, minced
2 tablespoons chopped fresh parsley
2 tablespoons chopped fresh cilantro
3 tablespoons balsamic vinegar
3 tablespoons red wine vinegar
1/2 cup olive oil

Combine all the ingredients. Cover and let stand for two hours in the refrigerator.

Makes 1 cup.

There are more than 200 varieties of chili peppers grown throughout the world.

Chili Apple Salsa

A great salsa for pork chops!.

2 tablespoons vegetable oil
1 large onion, diced fine
6 tart apples, unpeeled, cored, chopped
　　into small pieces
2 tablespoons molasses
2 tablespoons sugar
1 tablespoons lemon or lime juice
1 tablespoon vinegar
2 dried chipotle chilies, soaked in warm water
　　for an hour, seeded and diced fine
1 tablespoon cumin
2 teaspoons chopped fresh oregano

Heat oil in a large skillet over medium heat and
sauté the onions for two minutes. Add the
apples, cover and cook for 8 to 10 minutes,
stirring a couple of times. Add molasses, sugar
and lemon juice. Stir until blended.

Combine the vinegar and chilies in a food
processor and purée. Pour into a large mixing
bowl and add cumin and oregano. Mix thoroughly.
Add the apple-onion mixture; mix well.
Refrigerate for at least two hours, or overnight.
Makes 4 cups.

Serrano Chili Salsa

A word of warning: Remember that the serrano chili is one of the hottest of chilies with a rich, clean heat!

2 cups chopped ripe tomatoes
1 tablespoon minced onion
1 tablespoon oil
1 teaspoon dried basil leaves
1 tablespoon dried cilantro
2 serrano chilies, seeded and minced
1 tablespoon lime juice

Mix all ingredients well. Let stand at room temperature for at least one hour before serving.
Makes 2 cups.

Chipotle chilies are dried jalapeño chilies canned in adobo salsa. These may be purchased in supermarkets or specialty food stores. They are very hot.

Sloppy Joe Salsa

An adaptation of the traditional South American ground beef recipe for burrito filling makes this a quick and easy recipe for your family or a crowd.

1 cup chopped onion
2 tablespoons vegetable oil
3/4 pound ground beef
1 can (7 ounces) chopped green chilies
2 tablespoons canned sliced jalapeño chilies
1 can (15 ounces) tomato sauce

Sauté onions in oil until translucent. Add beef and cook until done. Add remaining ingredients and simmer for 15 minutes.

Serve hot in buns, over rice or over baked potatoes.

Makes 4 cups.

Cocktail Salsa

All you need is a large bowl of tortilla chips, warmed in the oven, and a glass or two or wine.

4 large ripe tomatoes, diced fine
1 can (4 ounces) diced green chilies
1 medium yellow onion, minced
1 clove garlic, minced
1/4 cup fresh lime juice
2 tablespoons fresh lemon juice
1/2 teaspoon salt
2 ripe avocados, pitted and diced fine
1 cup finely chopped cilantro

Mix all ingredients except avocado and cilantro in a bowl. Allow to sit at room temperature. Shortly before serving, fold in avocado and cilantro.

Makes 3 cups.

Chili-Apricot Salsa

8-12 firm ripe apricots, pitted and chopped
1 yellow or orange bell pepper, stemmed,
    seeded and chopped
2 fresh jalapeño chili peppers, stemmed,
    seeded and chopped very fine
2 tablespoons minced fresh cilantro
1/4 cup fresh lime juice
Salt

Mix apricots, yellow bell pepper, jalapeño peppers, cilantro and lime juice. Season with salt. Chill for at least one hour before serving.

Makes 2-1/2 to 3 cups.

Apricot-Avocado Salsa

1 cup chopped apricots
1/2 cup chopped ripe tomato
1/2 cup chopped avocado
2 tablespoons sliced green onion
2 tablespoons lime juice
1/2 teaspoon fresh grated lemon peel
1 teaspoon fresh snipped rosemary

In a glass bowl, combine the ingredients. Cover and chill in the refrigerator for at least one hour before serving.

Makes 2 cups.

Peachy Salsa

This is an American version of a recipe that was originally designed for mangoes in Cuba, where it was born.

2 ripe, but firm peaches, peeled, pitted and
    diced
1/2 medium red onion, peeled and minced
1/2 cup canned pineapple juice
1/4 fresh lime juice
1 tablespoon minced fresh ginger
1 teaspoon ground cumin
1 teaspoon ground coriander
1 teaspoon brown sugar
1/2 teaspoon salt
1/4 teaspoon cayenne pepper

Combine the peaches, onion and remaining ingredients in a bowl; mix lightly. Cover and refrigerate.

Makes 3 cups.

Cucumber Mango Salsa

Admittedly an unusual combination of ingredients, but it's good. Really, really good!

2 cups diced ripe mango
1 cucumber, peeled, seeded and diced
1/2 poblano chili, seeded and minced
1 jalapeño chili, seeded and minced
2 teaspoons minced fresh ginger
1/4 cup chopped cilantro leaves
1 tablespoon brown sugar
1/4 cup fresh lime juice
Salt and black pepper

Combine all of the ingredients in a bowl, and toss to mix. Refrigerate, covered, until served. Prepare an hour or so before serving for best flavor.

Makes 2 cups.

Fresh Strawberry Salsa

Summer is the time for this versatile salsa, which is equally good on pork, chicken or turkey, or served on crackers with cheese.

1 pint fresh strawberries, diced
4 plum tomatoes, seeded and diced
1 small red onion, diced
1 medium jalapeño, minced
Juice of 1 lime
2 garlic cloves, minced
1 tablespoon olive or vegetable oil

In a bowl, combine strawberries, tomatoes, onions and peppers. Stir in lime juice, garlic and oil. Cover and chill for two hours.

Makes 4 cups.

Mexico's Pineapple Salsa

From Southern Mexico comes this salsa that may be served with saltwater fish, such as tuna or halibut.

1 small, fresh pineapple, peeled, cored and cubed
1 small red onion, diced
1 medium red bell pepper, cored, seeded and diced
1 medium yellow pepper, cored, seeded and diced
1 jalapeño chili, seeded and minced
1 teaspoon ground coriander
1 teaspoon ground cumin
2 tablespoons lime juice
1 clove garlic, minced

Combine all the ingredients in a bowl. Cover and let stand in refrigerator for one to two hours before serving. Serve chilled.

Makes 2 cups.

Salsa Verde, Cooked

This green salsa is a classic in the Southwest. This version is quite mild, and best when used as a dip.

1 cup finely chopped onion
2 cloves garlic, minced
2 tablespoons oil
1/2 teaspoon cumin
6 Anaheim chilies, roasted*, seeded and diced
2 cups water

Sauté onion and garlic in oil until onion becomes translucent. Add cumin, chilies and water. Simmer for 20 minutes.

Makes 2 cups.

Hold the chilies over gas or electric heat with long-handled fork; or blacken on an oiled cookie sheet under the broiler.

Southwest Bean Salad

Make this one a couple of days in advance—it stores well. Serve with pita bread, quartered and toasted.

4 medium red bell peppers, seeded and
   chopped fine
1 cup chopped red onion
1 tablespoon minced garlic
2 tablespoons olive oil
1/3 cup white wine
1/2 teaspoon dried oregano
1 can (15 ounces) black beans, drained and
   rinsed
1 teaspoon bottled hot pepper sauce
1 tablespoon fresh lime juice
3 tablespoons chopped fresh cilantro
Salt and freshly ground black pepper

Sauté the peppers, onions and garlic in the olive oil in a pan over moderate heat until the vegetables just begin to soften, 3 to 4 minutes. Add the wine and oregano and continue to cook for 3 to 4 minutes longer, until tender.

Cool and stir in the beans, hot pepper sauce, lime juice and cilantro. Season to taste.

                    Makes about 5 cups.

Mango Cantaloupe Salsa

Serve with any grilled or barbecued saltwater fish.

2 ripe mangoes, diced
1 medium cantaloupe, diced
1 can (4 ounces) chopped green chilies
6 scallions, thinly sliced
1/4 cup chopped fresh cilantro
2 tablespoons fresh lime juice
Pinch cayenne pepper

Mix all ingredients in a bowl. Serve at once, or refrigerate for up to three days.

Makes 3 cups.

Hawaiian Ginger-Pineapple Salsa

1-1/2 cups diced fresh pineapple
1/2 cup pineapple juice
1 tablespoon minced fresh ginger
2 tablespoons minced green onion
1/4 cup fresh lime juice
1 teaspoon minced Anaheim chili pepper

Combine all ingredients; mix well. Refrigerate until ready to serve.

Makes 2 cups.

Dessert Salsas

Chocolate-Cherry Salsa

For a very special meal, this warm chocolate-cherry sauce is delicious over vanilla ice cream.

1-1/2 cups (16-ounce can) canned cherries
   (including liquid)
1/2 cup sugar
1/2 cup semi-sweet chocolate (melted)
1/2 cup Kirsch liqueur

Combine sugar and cherries in a saucepan and bring to boil over medium heat. Simmer gently for 10 minutes. Add melted chocolate and mix well. Stir in Kirsch. Serve over ice cream, or a simple pound cake or angelfood cake.

Makes 2-1/2 to 3 cups.

Chocolate-Coffee Salsa

8 ounces semi-sweet chocolate (melted)
2 tablespoons butter (melted)
1/4 cup brown sugar
1/4 cup instant (powdered) coffee
1/4 cup Kahlua liqueur

Add melted butter to melted chocolate. Stir in brown sugar and instant coffee, stirring constantly until melted and combined. Add Kahlua liqueur and serve warm over vanilla or coffee-flavored ice cream.

Makes 1-1/2 to 2 cups.

Summer Salsa

2 cups peeled and diced watermelon
1 navel orange, peeled and diced
1 cup strawberries, coarsely chopped
1 to 2 tablespoons lemon juice
1 tablespoon honey or sugar
1/8 teaspoon cayenne pepper

Mix all ingredients in a medium-sized bowl. Refrigerate at least one hour before serving. Serve over ice cream.

Makes 3 cups.

Raspberry Salsa

A classic raspberry sauce, wonderful over good vanilla ice cream.

2 cups frozen raspberries (1 pound)
4 tablespoons water (1/4 cup)
4 tablespoons sugar
1/4 cup raspberry liqueur

Heat raspberries, water and sugar. Bring to boil and cook gently for 10 minutes. Remove from heat. Add liqueur. Serve warm over ice cream.

Makes 2 cups.

Mandarin Orange Salsa

The lovely citrus flavor of this sauce enhances ice cream or sorbets and is delicious served over sliced bananas.

1 can (11 ounces) Mandarin orange segments
   (including juice)
1 cup orange marmalade
1/2 cup Brandy or orange liqueur

Combine Mandarin oranges and marmalade. Simmer gently for 10 minutes. Add liqueur. Serve over cake or ice cream.

Makes 2 to 2-1/2 cups.

93

Pineapple-Rum Sauce

May be served warm or cold as a dessert salsa over pound cake.

1 20-ounce can crushed pineapple in heavy
    syrup
2 tablespoons minced candied ginger
1/2 cup Rum

Combine ginger and pineapple (including syrup) in a medium saucepan. Cook over medium heat until bubbly. Add Rum and mix well.

Makes 2 cups.

Bourbon Peach Salsa

4 medium peaches, sliced (2-1/2 cups)
3/4 cup brown sugar
1/2 cup water
1/2 cup Bourbon
1/2 teaspoon cinnamon

Combine peaches, sugar, water and Bourbon. Bring to boil over medium heat. Cook 10 minutes. Add cinnamon. Serve warm or cold over ice cream or pound cake.

Makes 3 cups.

SOME OF OUR OTHER BOOKS...

Great Salsas! (this book) $ 7.95 plus $2 S&H

The Wine-Lover's Holidays Cookbook
Menus, Recipes & Wine Selections for Holiday
Entertaining all year long!
$ 9.95 plus $2 S&H

Pairing Wine with Food
Hundreds of entrées matched to American and
Canadian Wines, and much, much more
$ 8.95 plus $2 S&H

Cooking with Wine
86 American Winery Chefs Share 172 of Their Favorite
Recipes for Cooking with Wine and Pairing Wine with Food
$ 14.95 plus $3 S&H

The California Wine Country Cookbook
102 of America's Finest Winery Chefs Share 172 of Their
Best Recipes with You
$ 14.95 plus $3 S&H

The California Wine Country Herbs & Spices
Cookbook, New & Revised Edition
A Collection of 212 of the Best REcipes by 96 Winery Chefs
and Winemakers, Featuring Herbs & Spices
$ 14.95 plus $3 S&H

To order, call toll-free (800) 852-4890, fax (707) 538-7371, e-mail HoffPress@world.att.net, or write to Hoffman Press, P.O. Box 2868, Santa Rosa, CA 95405. We accept MasterCard, VISA, Discover and American Express credit cards.

Your money back if you're not delighted!